OCEAN BOOK

written by
Clare Beaton
with Rudi Haig

illustrated by
Clare Beaton

b small publishing
www.bsmall.co.uk

Oceans

mackerel

stingray

Oceans are huge masses of salt water which cover almost three-quarters of the Earth's surface. There are five oceans: Arctic, Atlantic, Indian, Pacific and Southern, as well as smaller seas such as the Mediterranean.

The billions of plants and animals that live in the ocean are different from those living in freshwater rivers and ponds. The oceans are very deep and it's only in recent years that scientists have started to explore the dark depths where thousands more creatures are waiting to be found.

Despite the huge size of the oceans they are all under threat from pollution created by the modern world. Oil spills, poisons from factories and now all kinds of plastic are killing off sea birds and animals. Already the danger is so great that ways are being found to get rid of plastic bottles and packaging.

You can help too by never leaving litter on a beach and carefully collecting any you find there and disposing of it properly.

carragheen (Irish moss)

cuvie (forest kelp)

2

Activities

Each topic in this book comes with a simple craft activity or yummy recipe for you to enjoy at home. Here are some helpful tips to get you started.

Materials

It's useful to have some materials ready such as cereal and tissue boxes, thicker card and card tubes for when you feel creative.

Several activities in this book use recycled items and perhaps you could think of some more ideas.

Templates

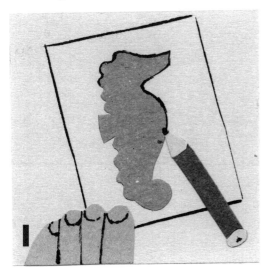

1 Place a piece of tracing paper over the template. Hold steady and draw around the shape.

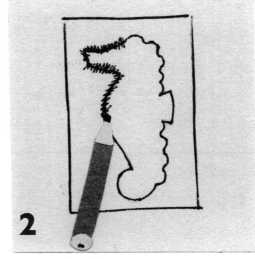

2 Turn the tracing paper over and scribble over the lines with a soft pencil.

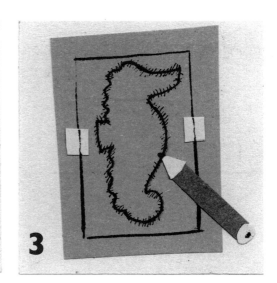

3 Turn over again and tape onto paper or card. Retrace firmly over the original lines. Remove tracing paper.

TIP You can use greaseproof paper instead of tracing paper.

Sharks

bull shark

hammerhead shark

Sharks have existed for a very long time, over 400 million years. They usually live in salty water and have fins and gills and snouts. There are about 500 species, or types of shark swimming in the oceans and they vary massively in size, shape, colour and behaviour. The biggest is the whale shark, about the size of a school bus.

The smallest is the dwarf lantern shark, which could fit in your hand. Great white sharks are the most famous species. Known for being impressive hunters, great whites can even jump really high into the air to catch their food.

leopard shark

great white shark

blue shark

Shark pop-up card

What you will need:
Piece of A4 paper, pencil, felt-tip pens, ruler, scissors.

1. Fold paper into four.
2. Open and draw a horizontal line 6.5 cm (2 ½ in) in the centre, 9 cm (3 ½ in) from the top.
3. Draw a zigzag across the line. Draw the outline and eyes of a shark.
4. Colour in the shark leaving the teeth white. Add waves if you like.
5. Open card completely and cut a slit along the line that you drew.
6. Fold card again and place forefinger into the slit pulling mouth up forming a triangle with the ends of the mouth and the top of the head. Close and press.
7. Open the card and repeat, pulling the bottom of the mouth down.

TIP You might want to practise making the opening mouth on some blank paper first.

basking shark

Ocean Floor

great scallop

common mussel

The ocean floor is home to lots of sea life, including over 5,000 species of crab. Some are as wide as cars, like the giant Japanese spider crab. While others are as small as peas, like the pea crab. All crabs have round shell bodies with two pincers, or claws and four pairs of walking feet that they use to move sideways.

Not all animals on the ocean floor have bones or shells. Anemones are colourful jelly-like creatures that look like lots of small fingers bunched together. They can stick to other objects and are poisonous, which means they can make animals or humans sick.

common lobster

anemone

common winkle

common grey sea slug

Toilet-roll crabs

What you will need:
Toilet roll card tube, two black buttons, masking tape,
glue, scissors, black felt-tip pen, orange paint and brush.

1. Cut tube into three pieces as shown.
2. Cut through one of the smaller rings,
   unfurl and cut ends into claws.
3. Cut through the other smaller ring,
   unfurl and cut 2.5 cm (1 in) off one
   end and discard. Then cut the ends
   into four points for the legs.
4. Slightly squash the large ring. Push
   the claws through and tape to the
   inside at the front.
5. Push the legs through and tape onto
   the inside at the bottom.
6. Paint it orange and leave it to dry.
7. Glue on buttons for eyes and
   draw a mouth.

hermit crab

limpet

7

Funny Fish

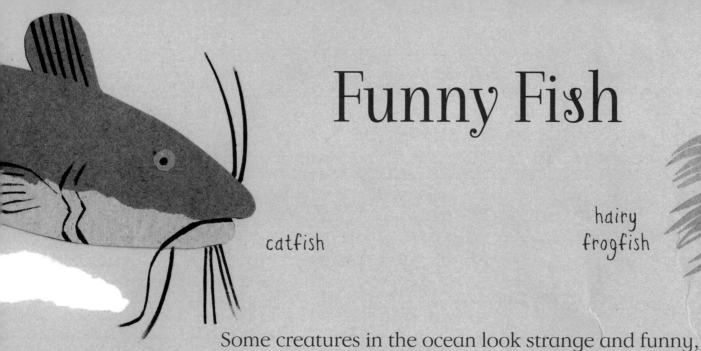
catfish

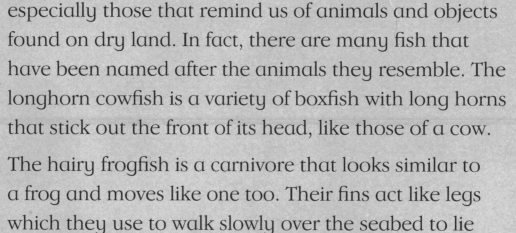
hairy frogfish

mousefish

Some creatures in the ocean look strange and funny, especially those that remind us of animals and objects found on dry land. In fact, there are many fish that have been named after the animals they resemble. The longhorn cowfish is a variety of boxfish with long horns that stick out the front of its head, like those of a cow.

The hairy frogfish is a carnivore that looks similar to a frog and moves like one too. Their fins act like legs which they use to walk slowly over the seabed to lie in wait for their prey.

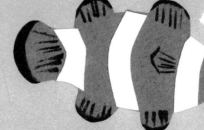
clownfish

longhorn
cowfish

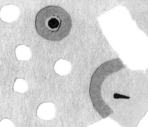

parrotfish

Colourful fish creations

Many fish have funny names such as the clownfish, cowfish, catfish, dogfish and parrotfish. There is even a hairy frogfish! Create these or think of some funny fish of your own.

What you will need:
Pencil and tracing paper, thick coloured or white paper, felt-tip pens, decorations such as sequins, glitter, stickers and wool, scissors, sticky tape and glue.

1. Trace the fish template onto paper (see instructions on page 3) and cut out.
2. Create your own funny fish decorating both sides.
3. Hang up with lengths of wool taped to the top, or tape at the bottom to thin sticks and stand them up in plant pots or modelling clay.

fish template

9

Luminous Creatures

Antarctic krill

Commerson's frogfish

bluebottle

anglerfish

deep sea worm

luminous brittle star

The world's oceans are very deep, in some places around 36,000 feet which is about how high up aeroplanes fly in the sky. It's very dark in these waters and many sea creatures are able to produce their own light down here. This is called bioluminescence.

Creatures glow and glitter for many reasons, like anglerfish that dangle a lighted lure in front of their mouths to attract prey to feed on. Or deep sea worms that produce different lights to communicate with each other. Bioluminescence can also be a form of protection used to scare and confuse any nearby predators.

Amazing sea creatures

What you will need:
Thin white card or thick white paper, black poster paint and a large brush, brightly coloured wax crayons and cocktail sticks.

1. Cover the card or paper in a thick layer of crayoning. Don't leave any white showing and use lots of colours.
2. Cover with a layer of black paint and leave to dry.
3. Using a cocktail stick, scratch through the paint drawing deep-sea creatures. Make them as amazing as you can!

1.

2.

3.

Dolphins and Porpoises

bottlenose dolphin

common dolphin

Dolphins and porpoises are large marine mammals that look alike and are mostly found in shallow seas. They are known for being very clever and for using sonar, or sound, to move around underwater.

Dolphins are usually grey in colour and have longer noses and bigger mouths than porpoises. They also have curved dorsal fins in the middle of their backs and leaner bodies. Porpoises, like the harbour porpoise, are often darker with a white or grey belly. They also have small pointed flippers and dorsal fins shaped like triangles. Dolphins are more talkative than porpoises, as they whistle through their blowholes to communicate underwater.

harbour porpoise

Porpoise or dolphin wheel

What you will need:
Large plate measuring about 20 cm (8 in) across or use
a compass, pencil and tracing paper to make one,
felt-tip pens or paint and brush, thick white paper, thin
blue card, scissors and one paper fastener.

1. Draw around the plate onto paper and cut out.
2. Trace the porpoise or dolphin templates (see
   instructions on page 3) onto the paper disc
   and colour in. Make them all swim in the same
   direction. If using paint, leave to dry.
3. Cut card into a rectangle measuring 30 cm x 20 cm (12
   in x 8 in) and cut one long edge into waves.
4. Push paper fastener through the top centre of the
   wavy edge of the card from the front and through
   the centre of the disc. Fold ends of fastener flat.

TIP: You could also make a whale or flying fish wheel.

dolphin template

porpoise template

13

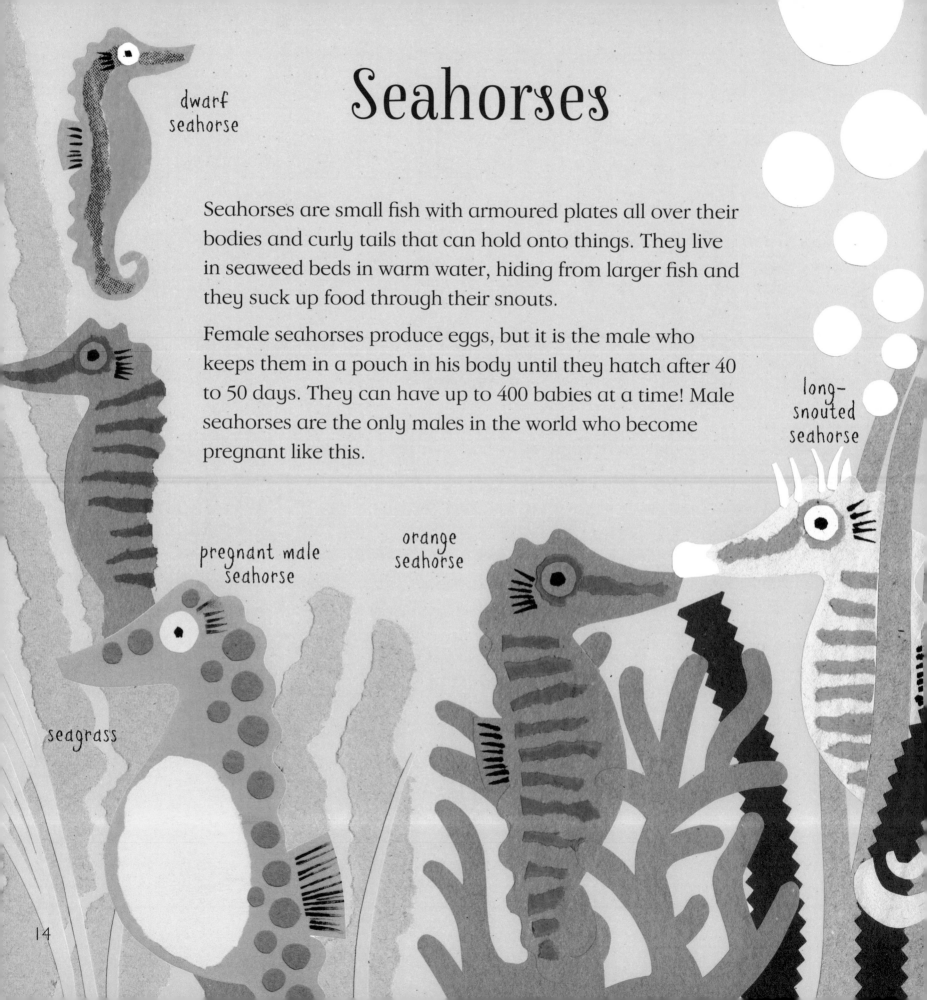

dwarf
seahorse

Seahorses

Seahorses are small fish with armoured plates all over their bodies and curly tails that can hold onto things. They live in seaweed beds in warm water, hiding from larger fish and they suck up food through their snouts.

Female seahorses produce eggs, but it is the male who keeps them in a pouch in his body until they hatch after 40 to 50 days. They can have up to 400 babies at a time! Male seahorses are the only males in the world who become pregnant like this.

long-
snouted
seahorse

pregnant male
seahorse

orange
seahorse

seagrass

Sparkly seahorse decoration

What you will need:
Felt, sequins, two small buttons, scissors, pins, glue, pencil and tracing paper, 10-cm (4-in) length of wool or thin ribbon.

1. Trace the seahorse template twice (see instructions on page 3). Pin onto two pieces of felt and cut around the shape through the paper and felt. Unpin the paper and discard.
2. Place the ends of the wool or ribbon on one seahorse head. Cover the whole seahorse with glue and place the second seahorse on top, pressing together.
3. Decorate both sides, gluing on the buttons for the eyes.
4. Leave to dry and hang up!

TIP: You can make your seahorse in one colour or two.

seahorse template

Starfish

Some of the most colourful creatures to be found on the ocean floor are starfish, or sea stars. There are around 1,500 species of starfish living in both warm tropical waters and cold polar oceans.

Most starfish have five arms, or rays, that come out from a central disk body. However, some types can have up to fifty rays. The purple sunstar can have between seven and thirteen rays.

Some starfish also have the special ability to regenerate, or grow back, their rays and other parts of their bodies if they get injured. This regrowth can take several months or years though.

starlet

dulse
(palmaria palmata)

common
starfish

purple sunstar

common
sunstar

goose foot
starfish

Starfish biscuits

What you will need:
225 g (8 oz) self-raising flour, pinch of salt (optional), 150 g (5 oz) butter, 125 g (4 oz) caster sugar, a beaten egg, bowl, baking trays, aluminium foil, five-point star biscuit cutter, wooden spoon, fork, cooling rack.

1. Sift the flour and salt into a bowl and rub the butter in finely. Add the sugar and beaten egg then mix to a stiff dough. Turn onto a lightly floured surface and knead until smooth. Cover in foil and chill in the fridge for 30 minutes.
2. Roll dough out quite thinly on a lightly floured surface and cut into stars. Place onto buttered baking trays and prick with a fork.
3. Bake in preheated oven 180° C (350° F) or Gas Mark 4 for about 12 minutes until golden. After a couple of minutes transfer to cooling rack.

Icing

What you will need:
225 g (8 oz) icing sugar, two tablespoons boiling water, yellow or orange food colouring, bowl, spoon and knife.

1. Put sugar in a bowl and gradually add the water and mix to a smooth thick consistency. Add a few drops of colouring and mix well.
2. Ice biscuits using a knife dipped in boiling water. Sprinkle with hundreds-and-thousands if you like, before the icing has set.

Seaweed servers

What you will need:
Seaweed coloured card, pencil and scissors.

Draw seaweed shapes on card and cut out. Arrange biscuits on them!

Nautical Flags

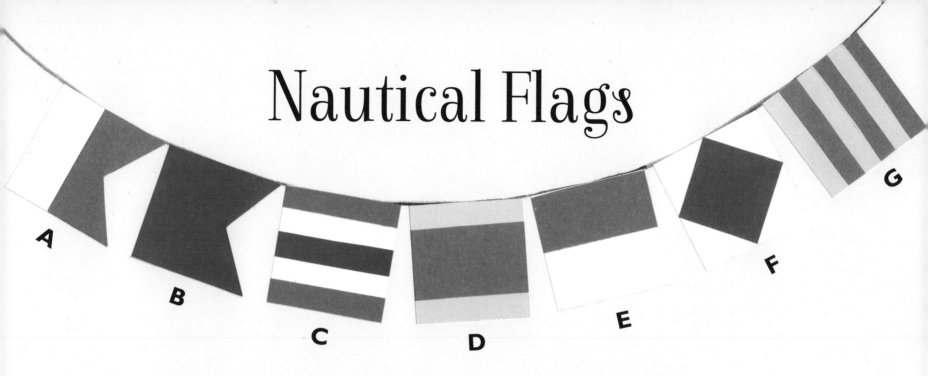

A B C D E F G

Nautical flags allow ships and boats to talk to one another. They also let ships communicate with people or places on shore. Nautical flags are made up of 26 square flags which stand for different letters of the alphabet. Ships can use them to spell out messages, or use a single flag whose 'letter' is code for a different meaning.

For example, the letter 'A' tells other ships to keep clear as there is a diver swimming underwater. Nautical flags are made up of colours that can be easily recognised at sea. These are red, blue, yellow, black and white.

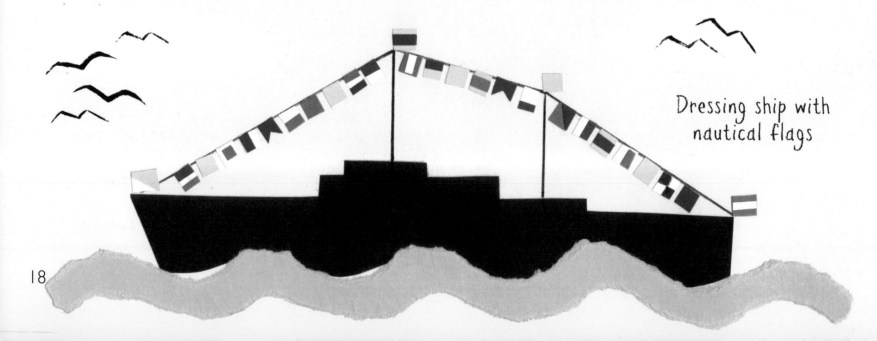

Dressing ship with nautical flags

The International Code of Signals

These flags are used by ships and boats to send messages to each other.

Make your own messages or greeting or write your name using the alphabet flags.

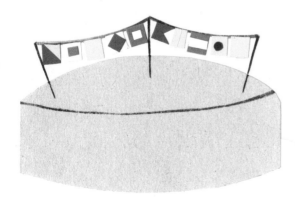

What you will need:
White paper, pencil and ruler, scissors, yellow, blue, red and black paint and brush or pens and crayons, string and sticky tape.

1. When you have decided on your word or words cut the paper into the number of squares you need. The size depends on what you are using them for, mini ones to decorate a cake and larger ones as a banner.
2. Using the ruler and pencil draw the patterns on the paper squares and colour in.
3. Tape onto string at the back leaving a length each end to hang up. You can make this horizontal or vertical.

Jellyfish

box
jellyfish

With umbrella-shaped heads, or bells, and flowing tentacles, jellyfish are some of the most recognisable animals found in the world's oceans. As their name suggests, jellyfish have soft jelly-like bodies which swim around by using their bells to pulsate, or move quickly back and forth.

Jellyfish range in size from about a fingernail to those like the lion's mane jellyfish whose bells can be over two metres wide, or as big as a van. Jellyfish tentacles are often full of painful stingers that can be used as defence or to catch food. This is why people need to be careful when swimming near jellyfish.

purple-striped
jellyfish

'pink meanie' jellyfish

moon jellyfish

lion's mane jellyfish

Jellyfish bowl decorations

What you will need:
White card bowl, coloured thin plastic (like a spare plastic bag or similar), sticky tape, scissors, glue and thin elastic.

1. Cut the plastic into thin strips.
2. Tape one end of each strip around the inside of the bowl. Cut some into different lengths.
3. Knot one end of elastic and push through the centre of the bowl from the inside and hang up.
4. Decorate the bowl by gluing on the plastic shapes.

TIP: You can make this into a hat by attaching the elastic to both sides of the bowl and knotting and cutting off to fit.

Ocean Boats

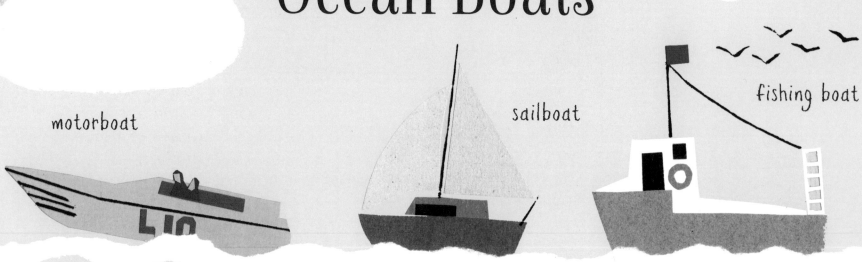

motorboat

sailboat

fishing boat

For people, the only way to travel long distances across seas and oceans without using an aeroplane is by boat. Sailboats use sails, or structures often made of fabric, to capture the power of the wind to move on water. Much bigger boats like ferries and cruise liners use man-made machines called engines to power their journeys.

Some boats also have jobs that they do like lifeboats, which help rescue passengers from boats caught in dangerous conditions like bad weather. Or tugboats that push or pull larger vessels that have broken down and those that need help moving through busy harbours or narrow canals.

lifeboat

tugboat

Boat hat

What you will need:
Piece of A2 paper, felt-tip pens, small piece of paper, sticky tape and a cocktail stick.

1. Fold paper in two. Fold top two corners over to meet in the centre. Fold up bottom strip and turn over and repeat. Smooth flat with hands. *
2. Make a small flag with paper and a cocktail stick and tape to the top of the sails.
3. Write name (and number if liked) on boat.

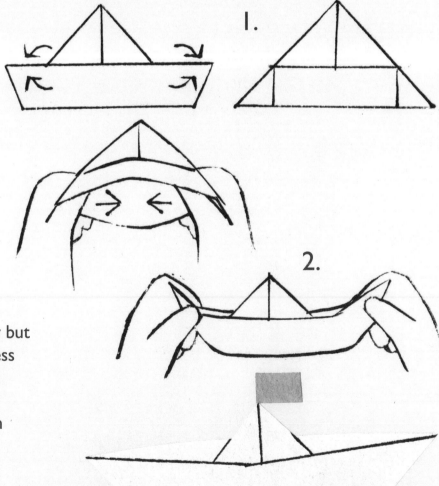

1.

2.

Paper boat

What you will need:
A4 piece of paper, felt-tip pens.

1. Fold as for **Boat hat** until * then fold the ends of the bottom strip over.
2. Place thumbs inside bottom of boat and turn strip upwards (as if turning inside out). This is a bit tricky but persevere! The boat will now have a double thickness of paper around the bottom. Place on a surface and smooth flat with hands.
3. Pull slightly apart to stand. You can write a name on the bottom and add a flag (see above) if you like.

TIP: You can use the small boats as snack 'bowls' or try sailing them.

Coral Reef

yellow
tang

harlequin filefish

Coral reefs are colourful underwater ecosystems. They are built from groups of living polyps, or tiny tube-shaped animals tightly packed together. These polyps let out a substance called calcium carbonate, which is also found in rocks and this causes them to become hard like stone.

Coral reefs are mostly found in shallow tropical waters and are home to many bright and colourful creatures including sea snakes and French angelfish. Unfortunately, many of the world's coral reefs are being destroyed by too much fishing, or rubbish being dumped into the water. People need to help save these reefs to protect the animals living there.

French angelfish

jewelled topsnail

sea
snake

Make your own coral reef

What you will need:
Card tubes, thin card, small box or lid of box, paints and brush, pencil and felt-tip pens, sequins and glitter, scissors and glue.

1. Paint tubes different colours, also paint the outside of the box or lid (which will be the base) and leave to dry.
2. Cut coral shapes out of card, paint both sides and leave to dry.
3. Draw and cut out fish from card. Colour and decorate both sides.

4. Stand the box or lid so the flat side is on top, arrange tubes on the surface drawing around each with the pencil. Cut out holes inside the line (so that the tubes fit firmly) and cut thin slits for the coral pieces. Push the tubes and coral carefully into the holes and slits.
5. Glue on the fish with some poking through the coral tubes. Glue on sequins and glitter when in position.

TIP: You can add more to your coral reef if you like such as shells and an octopus.

Beachcombing

Beachcombing is the act of visiting a beach when the tide is out to search for items of value or interest. It can also help with a 'beach clean', as you pick up bits of rubbish and plastic that have been littered. These can be recycled, or used for arts and craft creations.

As a beach is never the same from day to day, there could be almost anything that washes up. Maybe you'll even find a lump of rare and valuable ambergris, which is a smelly wax-like substance made by sperm whales that is used to make perfume.

Recycling fun

Next time you go for a walk along a beach take a bag with you and start collecting interesting things you might find. These could include smooth drift wood, plastic bits and pieces, nylon rope, shells with holes in them. Leave anything sharp and dirty or splintery wood.

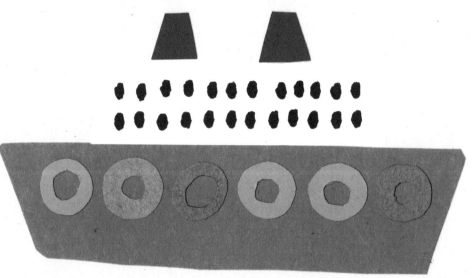

1. Rinse everything with cold water and leave to dry.
2. The things you have found will help you decide what to make. A bird on a branch, a small figure or a display remembering that day or holiday.
3. Use string, glue, paper clips or drawing pins to construct your found bits but these shouldn't show too much.
4. If making a display divide a card box or lid with card 'shelves' and arrange your best things on them. You can write when and where you found them.

TIP: As well as having fun creating something out of nothing you will have done some good by cleaning up the beach.

Penguins

Penguins are a group of birds that cannot fly. Usually found in colder climates, their evolution has seen their wings become flippers, which make them very strong swimmers. In fact, they spend about half their lives swimming in water, where they catch and feed on fish and squid. There are several species of penguin, each with unique appearances like the rockhopper penguin with its yellow feathered eyebrows. However, all penguins have black backs and wings with a white belly. This is a type of camouflage that helps protect them from predators like leopard seals, who find it more difficult to see them swimming.

rockhopper penguin

king penguin

African penguin

baby penguins

Paper cup penguins

What you will need:
Plastic or paper cups (you can rinse and dry used ones), black and white paint, brush, black and yellow paper, scissors, glue and sticky tape, black felt-tip pen, tracing paper and pencil.

1. Trace the wing and eye template twice and the beak once (also the eyebrows twice for the rockhopper penguin) onto black and yellow paper. See instructions on page 3 for how to trace.
2. Cut out wings, eyes and beak (eyebrows too, if wanted).
3. Paint cup or cups black and white. If the cups are white just paint the black part. Then leave to dry.
4. Push closed scissors into cup to make a small hole where the beak goes. Fold the beak cone into a point and secure with tape. Push, point first, through hole from the inside, leaving the end inside. There should be no need to secure with tape if the hole is small.
5. Glue wings onto sides pointing backwards from the front.
6. Finally draw a black dot in the centre of the eyes and glue in position. Add eyebrows if wanted.

TIP: If using plastic cups mix some liquid soap into the paint. This helps the paint stick to the plastic.

large penguin templates

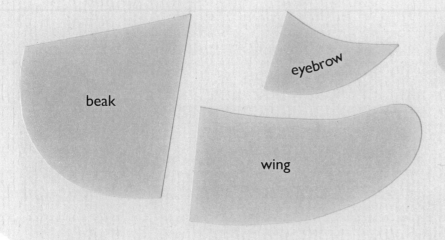

beak

eyebrow

eye

wing

beak

eyebrow

eye

wing

small penguin templates

Sea turtles

Sea turtles, or marine turtles, are reptiles found in every ocean except at the polar regions, which are too cold. They are much larger than normal turtles. They have a hard shell that acts as armour to protect them from predators. The top side of this shell is called the carapace.

There are seven different species of sea turtle, each with different shaped shells. The biggest species is the leatherback which can grow up to six feet long and weigh over 1,000 pounds. That's about the same as a horse. Sea turtles cannot breathe underwater but many can hold their breath for over thirty minutes.

turtle eggs and a baby turtle hatching

loggerhead turtle

leatherback turtle

green turtle

sea turtle template

Crafty sea turtle art

What you will need:
Large paper plate or stiff coloured or white paper, paints and brush or coloured papers, felt-tip pens, pencil and tracing paper, scissors, sticky tape.

1. Trace the template (see instructions on page 3), including slits.
2. Cut out turtle including slits and add markings in paint, cut-out paper or pens. Draw the eyes.
3. Overlap each side of the slits by a little under 1 cm (½ in) and secure underneath with tape.
4. Carefully bend the flippers downwards and stand up.

TIP: Look at the turtles opposite for different markings.

SLIT

SLIT

3.

baby leatherback turtle

shrimp

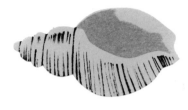
common whelk

Glossary

These difficult words appear in the book.
Here is what they mean.

ambergris – a wax-like substance made by whales

bioluminescence – the ability of living creatures to light up

calcium carbonate – white substance found naturally in chalk and shells

camouflage – an animal using its colour or shape to hide in its surroundings

carapace – a hard shell that covers and protects animals

carnivore – an animal that eats meat

dorsal fins – a fin located on an animal's back

ecosystem – all living things in an area affecting each other and their surroundings

evolution – the way living things change over millions of years

flippers – arm-like parts on sea creatures used for swimming

lure – something used to tempt an animal

mammals – animals, with fur or hair, that produce milk for their young

pincers – the claws of animals like crabs

polyps – small tube-shaped water animals

predators – animals that hunt and eat other animals

regenerate – to grow again

reptiles – cold-blooded animals with scaly skin that usually lay eggs

sonar – using sound waves to locate things

species – a group of plants or animals with similar features

Published by b small publishing ltd.
First published in 2019 by b small publishing ltd.
Ocean Book   ISBN 978-1-911509-85-1   www.bsmall.co.uk
text and illustrations © b small publishing 2019
Editorial: Sam Hutchinson   Design: Louise Millar   Production: Madeleine Ehm   Publisher: Sam Hutchinson
1 2 3 4 5 6 7 8 9

British Library Cataloguing-in-Publication Data:
A catalogue record for this book is available from the British Library.

sea fan

oyster